The Best Down~Home Recipes:

A Country Cooking Cookbook

Sandy Smith

DEDICATION

I am dedicating my thoughts and memories to my parents (Larry Smith & Margaret Webb), sister Linda Smith, my godparents (David & Sharon Logan), godbrothers (Curt & Darby) and my godsister (Lana Logan) and to the rest of my family and friends who made my writing come true. Thank you everyone who inspired my dreams.

CONTENTS

MAIN COURSES

Chicken Lasagna

As long you like/love casseroles like I do and most of the people that I know, this may be something that you may enjoy. The vegetables are optional. If you are trying to get your kids and other family to eat their vegetables, then this will be a good way to do it.

5 to 6 pieces of skinless boneless chicken breast, cooked and cut up
Salt and pepper
1 large onion, diced
1 large green pepper, diced
2 cans (15.25 ounce) corn, peas, or green beans, or a small bag of mixed vegetables, optional
1 24-ounce cottage cheese
1 package (8 ounce) shredded mozzarella cheese
1 jar (16 ounce) cheesy Ragu classic alfredo

1 package (8 ounce) oven-ready lasagna noodles
1 tbsp. basil

1. In a pan add the chicken, season with salt and pepper, and cook until done. Cut up and set aside.
2. Preheat oven to 350 degrees.
3. Cut up the onion and green pepper. Set aside.
4. Layer the lasagna noodles, add enough of the Ragu sauce, add the chicken, onion, green pepper, optional the vegetables, cottage cheese, sprinkle the cheese, add the last part of the lasagna noodles and whatever is left on the Ragu sauce. Cover with foil.
5. Bake for 45 to 50 minutes. Pull out of the oven, take the foil off, and put back into the oven for 5 to 10 more minutes (might even go the extra 15 minutes, depending on your oven).

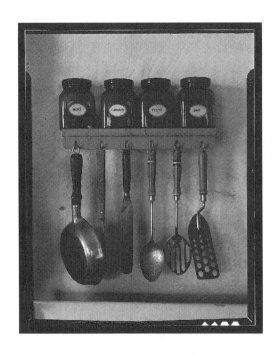

Mostaccioli Pizza

You can use any type of pasta in this recipe except spaghetti thins. You can use pizza sauce if you want. Or, you can use pizza sauce instead of using mozzarella and cheddar cheese.

1 package mostaccioli pasta
1 jar spaghetti sauce
1 1/2 pounds ground beef
1 pound Italian sausage or pork sausage, optional
1 medium onion, sliced
1 medium green pepper, sliced
mozzarella cheese
cheddar cheese
1 package pepperoni slices
anything you want to add

1. Preheat oven to 350 degrees.
2. Cook pasta according to the box. Drain well. Brown beef and sausage. Drain well.
3. In a 9x13 inch pan, layer pasta, spaghetti sauce, beef mixture, onion, green pepper, and any other ingredients you want to add, such as cheeses or pepperoni. Cover with aluminum foil. Bake for 20 to 25 minutes.

Sandy's Meatloaf

1 1/2 pounds ground beef
1 medium onion, diced fine
1 medium green pepper, diced fine
6 sticks of celery, chopped fine (optional)
2 to 4 eggs
1 can (14.5 oz) tomato sauce
1 1/2 cups bread crumbs
1/2 teaspoon salt and pepper (Each)
1/2 teaspoon garlic powder
ketchup

1. Preheat oven to 350 degrees.
2. In an mixing bowl combine the first nine ingredients. Mix well.
3. In a pan add the meat. Zig zag the ketchup. Bake for 45 minutes or until no more pink in the middle.

Sandy's Spinach Pasta

2 Polish sausages, sliced
1 small onion, diced
water
1 to 1 1/2 cups elbow macaroni
1 can (13.5 ounce) spinach, undrained
1 can (10 ounce) diced tomatoes with green chilies
1 can (8 ounce) tomato sauce
1 teaspoon garlic powder
1 teaspoon meat tenderizer
3 hard-boiled eggs, diced
mozzarella cheese
Miracle Whip or mayo, optional

1. In an big sauce pan add the sausages and onion. Fry them up until the onion is lightly browned. Then add enough water to cook the elbow macaroni. Let it come to a boil. Add the elbow macaroni. Boil and stir according to the package. Drain well.
2. Add the spinach, diced tomatoes with green chilies, tomato sauce, garlic powder and meat tenderizer. Cook till there is no more juice. In an bowl add the food. Sprinkle cheese to your liking.

Rodeo Burger

I (Sandy) used to work at Burger King. When they had this on the menu that I thought that I'd would make my own version.

1 package hamburger buns
1 1/2 pounds ground beef
salt and pepper
3 to 4 onion rings per hamburger (depending on the size)
1 slice American cheese per hamburger
barbecue sauce
Miracle Whip or mayo
mustard (optional)
pickles (optional)

1. Brown the ground beef and season with salt and pepper. Add the hamburgers onto a plate till completely done.
2. Follow the instructions from the onion rings. (I tend to brown mine in the oven and use the temp. for the oven and bake for 7 minutes on each side).
3. On the top of the bun add Miracle Whip or mayo and sliced cheese. Add the barbecue sauce, onion rings and the hamburger then add the bottom bun. Optional mustard and pickles.
What I tend to do. As I have the hamburgers in the skillet, I add the barbecue sauce and the cheese on each one of the hamburger and then once the cheese is melted, I tend to put the hamburgers onto two folded paper towels folded up to let the grease come off the hamburgers. In the process that I add my Miracle Whip on the top bun and the three onion rings, the hamburger and the bottom bun.

Sassy Meatballs

1 1/2 pounds ground beef
1/3 pound Italian sausage or pork sausage
1 small onion, diced fine, or 1 package onion soup mix
1 small green pepper, diced fine (optional)
2 tablespoons finely chopped fresh parsley (optional)
1 small can tomato paste, tomato sauce, or 1/2 cup tomato juice
or V8 juice
1/2 cup bread crumbs or 6 pieces bread (When using bread, tear
into pieces), to your liking
1/2 teaspoon liquid smoke or Worcestershire sauce
1 package crackers, crushed
1 or 2 eggs
oil of your choice for frying

1. In a big enough bowl mix the ten ingredients together. Mix
well. Form the meat into walnut-size balls.
2. Heat the oil until it's very hot in a large frying pan. Fry the
meatballs for 5 to 7 minutes or to a golden brown. Drain well on
paper towels.
3. Serve with barbecue sauce or anything you desire.

If you don't want to fry the meatballs, bake them in the oven at
350 degrees for 30 minutes. Or, you can cook them in a crock
pot for 7 to 8 hours.

Dressing

24 pieces bread
2 medium or 1 large onion, diced fine
3 sticks celery, diced (may need more)
3 eggs
rubbed sage to taste
broth from turkey

1. Toast the bread and tear into pieces and put into an large bowl.
2. In the same bowl with the toasted bread add the diced onion, celery, eggs and by taste of sage and broth from the turkey. Mix well.
3. In an 8x8 or 9x9 inch pan. Pour the dressing into the pan.
4. Preheat oven according to the temperature you bake the turkey at, and bake the dressing for 15 to 20 minutes.

Shandi Hart

Mini Hamburgers

1 1/2 pounds ground beef
1 medium onion, diced
8 to 10 pieces of bread, torn into pieces OR use 3/4 cup bread crumbs
salt and pepper to season
vegetable oil

In an mixing bowl combine ground beef, onion and bread or bread crumbs. Mix well. Roll into medium size balls.
Add enough oil to the bottom of a skillet, just enough to cover the bottom. When the skillet is hot, add the hamburgers and season with salt and pepper. Fry on both sides till they are golden brown.

Kodie M. Masoner and Shandi Hart

Potato Chip Casserole

1 bag (12 ounce) Lay's plain potato chips, crushed (we get the family size bag)
1 can (10.5 ounce) cream of mushroom soup
1 can regular milk
5 cans (5 ounce) tuna, drain the liquid

1. Preheat oven to 350 degrees.
2. In an bowl stir together cream of mushroom soup and milk. Wish well.
3. Lightly spray the casserole dish. Layer potato chips, then layer in an half-can of tuna and cream and mushroom soup mixture, and repeat twice more.
Bake for 45 minutes.

Pizza Burgers

1 package hamburger buns
1 squeeze bottle or jar of pizza sauce
1 package shredded cheddar cheese
1 1/2 pounds ground beef
salt and pepper

1. Preheat oven to 350 degrees.
2. Brown ground beef and season with salt and pepper. Drain the excess fat.
3. Split the buns, add enough pizza sauce to spread around the bun, add ground beef to your liking, and sprinkle cheese on top.
4. Bake for 10 minutes (That's on an air bake sheet).

Spinach Lasagna

1 can spinach or bag spinach
1 1/2 pounds ground beef
salt and pepper
1 can (26.5 ounce) or jar (24 ounce) spaghetti sauce
1 container (24 ounces) cottage cheese
1 package shredded mozzarella cheese
1 package shredded cheddar cheese
parmesan cheese, optional
oven ready lasagna noodles
other ingredients to your desire

1. Preheat oven to 350 degrees.
2. Brown the ground beef, season with salt and pepper. Drain the excess fat.
3. In an 9x13 inch pan layer the noodles, spaghetti sauce, ground beef, spinach (when using can spinach, squeeze the spinach to get the juice out), cottage cheese, both cheeses, optional parmesan cheese and top with the lasagna noodles. As long that you have extra spaghetti sauce add the extra sauce on top on the noodles. Cover with foil. Bake for 45 minutes or to your desire. Pull foil off and bake for another 15 to 20 minutes longer or to your desire.

Sausage Egg Cheese Biscuit Sandwich

I've been told this is like store-bought.

1 container of 10 biscuits
1 package of sausage
4 eggs
2 slice cheese

1. Follow the instructions from the packages of the biscuits and sausage. Bake the biscuits and cook the sausage.
2. Fry the eggs and cut them into half.
3. Take the biscuits out of the oven and let them cool a little. Cut a biscuit in half. On the biscuit, add sausage, half the egg, part of the cheese, and the top biscuit.

Tater Tot Taco Ravioli Bake

Could microwave this as well with the same amount of time (30 minutes)

1 1/2 pounds ground beef
1 medium onion, diced fine
salt and pepper
1 package taco seasoning mix
2 cans (15 oz.) beef ravioli
shredded cheddar cheese
1/2 bag of tater tots

1. Preheat oven to 350 degrees.
2. Brown the onion, add ground beef and brown that, then season with salt and pepper. Drain the excess fat. Stir in the taco seasoning.
3. In an 9 x 9 or 9 x 13 inch pan, layer the tater tots, one can of ravioli, the ground beef mixture, and the last can of the ravioli. Sprinkle cheese to your liking, then layer the last round of tater tots. Bake for 30 minutes.

Beef Pie

1 1/2 pounds ground beef
1 package Lipton onion mix
1 can fried rice or 2 cups of La Choy chow mein noodles

1. Brown the ground beef and drain the excess fat.
2. Stir in the onion soup mix and fried rice or la chow noodles.
Cook for 5 minutes or longer.

Hearty Country Breakfast

1 loaf of frozen bread dough
bacon
sausage meat
ham
4 eggs
mozzarella cheese & cheddar cheese
onion (optional)

Unthaw overnight a loaf of frozen bread dough. In the morning take it out of the fridge and pull it out to fit a pizza pan. While the dough is warming, cook some bacon till crisp, and fry some sausage meat. Can use ham too – one or all of the meats.
Scramble about 4 eggs and put the cooked eggs on the dough. Sprinkle with mozzarella cheese & cheddar cheese if you have it. Then crumple bacon on top, some sausage & ham. I add onion on it top if you like onion.
Cook at 450 degrees until eggs are done & cheese melts.

Peggy Downs

Little Pizzas

English muffins
oil
pizza sauce
pepperoni
sausage
ham
pineapple
cheese

For a quick supper or lunch pizza, brush muffins with oil, put pizza sauce on them, then put pepperoni, sausage, ham and pineapple. Sprinkle cheese on top. Mozzarella is good.
They are fast & good. Bake in oven 375 degrees about 10 minutes.

Salisbury Steak In Mushroom Soup

1 ½ pounds ground beef
2 eggs
½ onion, diced or 1 package onion soup mix
½ teaspoon salt
¼ teaspoon black pepper
¼ cup V8 juice
1 ½ packages cracker crumbs
1 can cream mushroom soup
1 can regular milk

1. Preheat oven to 300 to 350 degrees.
2. In a big bowl mix the first 7 ingredients together well. Shape them into egg-sized balls. Brown the patties in an skillet on both sides. Set aside.
3. In another big enough bowl mix together the soup and milk. Set aside.
4. In an 9x13 inch pan add the patties, pour the soup over all, and let it cook for 30 to 35 minutes or until done.

Pigs In The Blanket

1 container of biscuits
1 sliced cheese
1 package hot dogs

1. Preheat oven according to the biscuits.
2. Take a biscuit and smash it flat. Add a quarter-piece of the cheese (one piece of cheese and fold into four), add the cheese on the biscuit and add the hot dog. Add the hot dog at the edge of the biscuit and roll. Bake according to the package. Don't overbake.

Beanie Weenies

Sprinkle enough brown sugar and enough (zig zag) ketchup to your liking.

1 package (12 oz) hot dogs
1 can (15 oz) pork and beans
1/4 cup brown sugar
1/4 cup ketchup

Open the pork and beans and pour them into the saucepan. Add the brown sugar and ketchup. Cut the hot dogs and add to the pork and beans. Mix well. Cook for 7 to 10 minutes.

Shandi Hart

Chicken and Noodles

3 pieces of chicken
1 to 1 1/2 cups egg noodles
2 instant bouillon chicken cubes
water
salt and black pepper
butter

In a large pan, add the chicken, enough water to cover the chicken, then season with salt, pepper and a spoon of butter. Let it come to a boil. Once it comes to a boil bring out the chicken and cut to your liking. Put back into the boiling water and boil for an extra 15 to 20 minutes. Add the chicken cubes and egg noodles. Cook the noodles according to the package.

Shandi Hart

2 cups (2 8-oz. cans) tomato sauce
½ cup water
3 cups cooked spaghetti
1 ½ cups diced leftover meat
½ lb. package Bordens Chateau, aka Velveeta, or two cups
shredded cheese
salt and pepper

Mix tomato sauce and water. Arrange alternate layers of
spaghetti, sauce, and cheese in greased 2-qt. baking dish, making
top layer cheese. Season with salt and pepper. Bake in moderate
oven (350 F.) 25 minutes. Serves 4-5.

Saucepan Spaghetti

Use your own ingredients when making this sauce. You can add whatever you want.

1 pound Italian sausage or pork sausage
1 1/2 pounds ground beef
3 1/2 cups water
1 can (15 ounce) tomato sauce
1 small onion, diced fine
1 small green pepper, diced fine (optional)
3 to 6 jalapenos, diced fine (optional)
1/2 teaspoon salt
1/4 to 1/2 teaspoon black pepper
1/4 teaspoon garlic powder
1/2 teaspoon liquid smoke or Worcestershire sauce
1 package (6 ounce) spaghetti thins or your choice of noodles
shredded cheddar cheese
other ingredients to your liking

1. Cook the meat in a big saucepan. Drain the excess fat.
2. In another saucepan combine water, tomato sauce, onion, optional green pepper, jalapenos, salt, pepper, garlic powder, liquid smoke or Worcestershire sauce, and other ingredients to your desire. Put it on high and bring to a boil, then add the spaghetti or your choice of noodles. Turn burner to low heat. Put the lid on the saucepan and let it simmer for 30 minutes. Stir often.
3. When the noodles are cooked, set aside. Add the sauce to the meat. Mix well. Serve, sprinkled with cheese.

Note: You can use the sauce without the meat and the spaghetti or your choice of noodles and dip breadsticks or whatever you want to dip with the sauce.

Julie Powell Casey

Chili

3 pounds hamburger
black pepper
2 to 3 cans stewed tomatoes
2 to 3 cans chili beans
2 medium minced onions
2 to 3 teaspoons chili powder
crackers

Brown hamburger, season with pepper. Drain the excess fat. Add stewed tomatoes, chili beans, minced onions (could brown the onions with the hamburger) and chili powder. Cook till it's heated. Take off the heat. In a bowl add chili and enough crackers to your liking. Cheese or sour cream is also very good.

Roast

1 to 2 pounds boneless loin roast
6 medium potatoes, cubed
2 pounds carrots, sliced and make as sticks
1 medium onion, sliced
salt and pepper
garlic powder
seasoning salt
2 cubes beef bouillon cubes
water

1. In a crock pot add the roast, season with salt, pepper, garlic powder, seasoning salt, beef cubes, onion, potatoes, carrots and a little bit of water to the bottom.
2. Cook for 8 hours or till ready to eat.
3. Slice and serve.

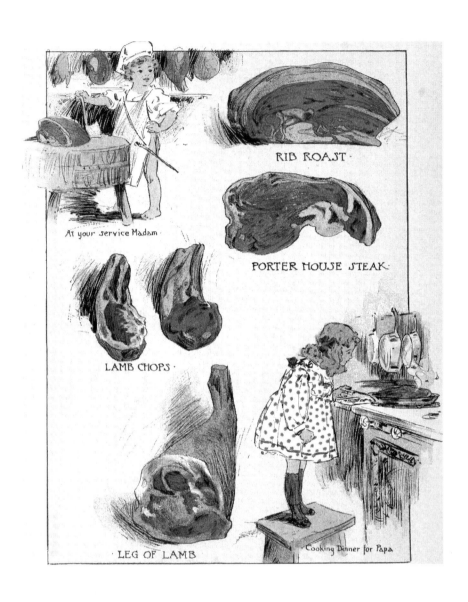

RIB ROAST·

At your service Madam·

PORTER HOUSE STEAK·

LAMB CHOPS·

·LEG OF LAMB

Cooking Dinner for Papa

Loose Hamburgers

1 1/2 pounds ground beef
1 small or medium onion, diced fine
seasoning
salt and pepper
pickles
mustard
Miracle Whip
ketchup
sliced cheese
hamburger buns

1. Brown the beef and onion. Drain the excess fat. Season to your liking.
On an hamburger add the beef and your add on's.
2. You can melt a slice of cheese on the bun or on the hamburger for extra goodness.

Meatball Sandwiches

homemade or store-bought meatballs
hamburger buns
shredded cheddar cheese or sliced cheese
homemade or store-bought spaghetti sauce
Miracle Whip or mayo

1. Preheat oven to 350 degrees.
2. On the bottom bun add spaghetti sauce, meatballs, and cheese.
3. Put the sandwich on an 9x13 baking pan. Bake for 5 to 10 minutes or until cheese is melted.
4. Add Miracle Whip or mayo on the top bun and put on top of the meatballs.

Macaroni And Cheese with Polish Sausages

This is a dish that I learned from Chris. It is very good and it is very easy to make.

4 Polish sausages
water
1 box macaroni and cheese

1. Cut the sausages. In a pan add the sausages and a tablespoon of water to the pan. Fry the sausages until browned.
2. Fill a saucepan with water. When it comes to a boil add the macaroni. Cook for 7 to 10 minutes. Drain.
3. Add whatever the measuring calls on the margarine or butter and milk. Stir the Polish sausages into the macaroni and cheese. Serve.

Shandi Hart, Shirley Shipley, Kelly Cline, Kodie M. Masoner and Melleigha Nichols

Salmon Patties

1 can pink salmon, make sure to take out the bones out
1 package crushed crackers
1 egg
vegetable oil

1. In a medium mixing bowl combine salmon, crackers and the egg. May need just an little bit more crackers but not much, just to make it moist.
2. Make them as four hamburger patties.
3. In a skillet add vegetable oil and the patties and fry till they get golden brown on both sides.

Candy Yams

2 cans (15 ounce) yams, drain juice from the second can of yams
1/2 cup brown sugar or to your liking
1 stick butter
1 bag (10 ounce,)mini marshmallows

1. Preheat oven to 350 degrees.
2. Add the yams. Make sure to drain the juice from the second can of yams. Sprinkle enough of the brown sugar. Slice the butter a quarter inch and add to the yams. Add the mini marshmallows. Bake for 15 to 20 minutes or until marshmallows are brown.

Shandi Hart

Green Bean Casserole

Tater tots
hamburger
shredded cheese
green beans
cream mushroom soup

1. Preheat oven to 350 degrees.
2. Brown the ground beef. Drain the excess fat.
3. In a bowl add the cream mushroom soup.
4. In an 9x13 inch pan layer the tater tots, add the ground beef, the cream mushroom and the green beans. Cover with foil. Bake for 45 minutes. Pull out the oven and take off the foil and bake for extra 5 to 15 minutes (depending on your oven).

I layer mine with tater tots, hamburger, shredded cheese, green beans, and cream of mushroom soup.

Shandi Hart

Pepperoni Meatball Stuffed Shells

1 package of jumbo pasta shells
1 jar (26 ounce) spaghetti sauce or your favorite pasta sauce

Sandy's Meatballs:
1 1/2 pounds ground beef
2 eggs
1/2 cup bread crumbs (optional)
1 medium onion, diced fine or 1 package Lipton Onion Soup Mix (I prefer the onion mix because it brings the flavor out in the meatballs)
1/2 teaspoon Worcestershire sauce or liquid smoke (optional)
1/2 teaspoon garlic powder
1/4 cup milk
1 package crackers, crushed
1 package pepperoni slices
1/2 cup shredded mozzarella cheese
1/2 cup shredded cheddar cheese

1. Preheat oven to 350 degrees.
2. In an mixing bowl add ground beef, eggs, optional bread crumbs, onion or Lipton onion mix, optional Worcestershire sauce or liquid smoke, garlic powder, milk and crackers. Mix well and shape into walnut-size balls. Should get roughly around 36 to 40 meatballs. Bake for 25-30 minutes.
3. Place 1/2 cup of the sauce in a 9x13 baking dish.
4. Cook the pasta according to the package directions, drain and let cool.
5. Place pepperoni and meatball in each shell and transfer to

prepared dish.

6. Top with the remaining sauce and sprinkle with the cheese. Cover with foil and bake for 15 minutes and take the foil off and bake for 10 minutes.

Ham and Cabbage

2 1/2 pounds Farmland ham, sliced
1 head of cabbage, sliced and cut
7 to 8 medium potatoes, peeled and sliced
8 cups of water

1. In a large pot put all the ingredients together.
2. Cook till the potatoes are tender.

DELICIOUS SALADS

Garden Salad

Here's a recipe that I came up with on my own.

1 onion, diced
1 green pepper, diced
1 cucumber, sliced
1 tomato, diced (optional)
1 lettuce, chopped (a bag salad is also fine)
1 pound cheddar cheese or shredded cheddar cheese
1 piece of chicken, smoked sausage, ham or turkey
salad dressing, Miracle Whip, or mayo
bacon bits (optional)
hard-boiled eggs

1. Cook the chicken, sausage, ham or turkey.
2. Chop up the lettuce, or pour a bag of salad, into a big bowl. Add onion, green pepper, cucumber, tomato, and cheddar cheese (When using the shredded cheddar cheese, wait till the

last minute and sprinkle enough of the cheese to your liking when adding to the salad).

3. Chop up the meat to a size of your liking. Set it aside until you're ready to serve the salad.

4. When it's time to serve the salad, put the salad in dishes, sprinkle with cheese, then lay meat on top. Ready to serve.

Macaroni Salad

2 cups elbow macaroni
9 to 10 eggs
1 large onion, diced
½ cup sweet pickle relish or to your liking
1 cup miracle whip or mayo or to your liking
1 teaspoon celery seed
Paprika, optional

1. Boil about 5 cups water. Once it comes to a boil, add the macaroni. Boil for 9 to 10 minutes.
2. In another pan, boil water, add the eggs, and let bubble for 10 to 15 minutes.
3. When the eggs are hard-boiled, run cold water over them to stop them from cooking.
4. Once the macaroni and eggs are cooled off, add them to a bowl and add the rest of the ingredients. Mix well.

MEASUREMENTS

Have you ever wondered about the measurements on things? This is a "BIG HELP" for people that I know. I hope it helps you.

16 1/2 cups all-purpose flour ~ 5 pound bag
25 3/4 cups sugar ~ 10 pound bag
4 1/3 cups brown sugar ~ 2 pound bag
8 1/2 cups powdered sugar ~ 2 pound bag
2 cups peanut butter ~ 18 oz., 1 lb., 2 oz.
17 3/4 cups rice crispies ~ 18 oz., 1 lb., 2 oz.
16 cups rolled oats ~ 42 oz., 2 lb., 10 oz.
7 3/4 cups elbow macaroni ~ 32 oz. bag (2 lbs.)
10 cups wide egg noodles ~ 16 oz. bag (1 lb.)
2 cups dry bread crumbs ~ 1 pound

TASTY DESSERTS

Chocolate Crinkle Cookies

These cookies are a hit with my family and friends.

6 eggs
3 cups sugar
8 ounces (1 box) unsweetened chocolate
1 cup vegetable oil
4 teaspoons baking powder
4 teaspoons vanilla
4 cups all-purpose flour
Sifted powdered sugar

1. In an big enough bowl mix together sugar, flour and baking powder. Melt the unsweetened chocolate and vegetable oil. Pour the chocolate mixture over the dry ingredients. Mix well. Add the vanilla and add one egg at a time while mixing. Cover and chill the dough overnight.
2. Preheat oven to 375 degrees. Shape the dough into balls and roll them into the powdered sugar. Bake for 8 to 10 minutes.

Chocolate Peanut Butter Oatmeal Bars

1 cup butter or margarine, softened
1 cup packed brown sugar
1 cup sugar
1 1/2 cups creamy peanut butter
2 eggs
2 teaspoons vanilla
1 1/2 cups all-purpose flour
2 cups quick oatmeal
2 teaspoons baking soda
2 teaspoons baking powder
1/2 teaspoon salt
1 package (12 oz.) mini chocolate chips or 10 oz. Reese's peanut butter chips

1. Preheat oven to 350 degrees.
2. In an mixing bowl cream together butter or margarine, both sugars and peanut butter. Mix well. Add eggs and vanilla. Mix well. In a separate bowl, combine flour, oatmeal, baking soda, baking powder and salt.
3.Lightly spray an 9x13 inch pan. Sprinkle the chips over the dough. Bake for 25 to 30 minutes or till golden brown around the edges. Cool completely.

Variation - To Make These Cookies Extra Special:
Add 1 1/2 cups flaked coconut. You can also use rice crispies to replace the rolled oats.

Graham Cracker Crusted Pudding Squares

When I came up with this recipe at the Saint Joseph Public Downyown Library in Saint Joseph, Missouri, I couldn't think of a name for this. Thank you, Melissa Penrod, for your help on the name for this recipe.

2 boxes graham crackers
4 boxes instant pudding
4 cups milk
1 tub cool whip
Chocolate syrup
Candy of your choice, optional

1. In an 9x13 inch or smaller pan, layer the graham crackers. Set aside what's left.
2. In an big enough bowl, add the pudding and the milk. Whisk well. Pour over the crackers. Add the cool whip and zig zag the chocolate syrup to your liking and optional candy of your choice. Could crush a package of graham crackers and add to the top. Refrigerate for 4 to 6 hours or overnight.

M&M Cookies

1 cup (2 sticks) butter or margarine, softened
1 1/2 cups sugar
1 1/2 cups brown sugar
2 to 3 medium or large eggs
3 cups all-purpose flour
1 teaspoon baking soda
1 teaspoon baking powder
1 1/2 cups M&M's

1. Preheat oven to 350 degrees.
2. In a large mixing bowl mix sugar, brown sugar, butter and eggs. Mix well. Stir in the remaining ingredients. Drop by tablespoons onto lightly sprayed baking sheets.
3. Bake for 10 to 12 minutes or until lightly brown around the edges.

Oreo Cheesecake

Here is a recipe that I came up with in my head after doing my own research on group recipes. This is my version.

2 6-ounce Oreo pie crusts
1 package (8 ounce) cream cheese, softened
1 1/2 cups sugar
1 cup all-purpose flour
2 eggs
3 teaspoons imitation vanilla flavor
16 Oreo cookies, crushed fine
1 tub (8 ounce) whipped topping
12 cookies to top it off

1. Preheat oven to 350 degrees.
2. Beat cream cheese, sugar, flour, eggs, and vanilla until everything is mixed. Add the crushed Oreo cookies and mix by hand. Add the filling evenly to each pie. Bake for 10 to 15 minutes or until the top is golden brown. Let the pies cool.
3. Once cooled, add half of the whipped topping to each pie and add 6 cookies to each pie. Refrigerate till ready to serve.

Peanut Butter Cookies

I (Sandy) found this recipe in a cookbook. The thing is that I made this recipe my way. Every time that I tend to make these cookies at the holidays, it seems like every one that I know tends to "LOVE" these. My family and friends tells me that these cookies are so soft and moist when they eat these cookies, that they can't have just one cookie!

1 ½ cups (3 sticks) butter, softened
1 ½ cups creamy peanut butter
1 ½ cups sugar
1 ½ cups packed brown sugar
1 ½ teaspoons baking soda
1 ½ teaspoons baking powder
3 eggs
1 ½ teaspoons vanilla
3 ¾ cups all-purpose flour
Granulated sugar

1. In a large mixing bowl beat together butter and peanut butter with an electric mixer on medium to high speed for roughly 30 seconds. Add in the sugar, brown sugar, baking soda and baking powder. Beat until combined by scraping the sides of the bowl. Beat in the eggs and vanilla until combined. Beat in as much of the flour mixture as you can with the mixer. Stir in an remaining flour. Cover the dough in an large bowl. Add the lid onto the bowl and refrigerate the dough overnight.
2. Preheat oven to 375 degrees.
3. In an medium bowl add about a cup of granulated sugar.

Shape the dough into balls (into 1 inch balls). Roll the dough into the sugar to coat. Place the dough onto an ungreased cookie sheet 2 inches apart. Flatten the dough with the tines of a metal fork by making crisscross on the dough. Bake for 7 minutes or until bottoms are light brown. Remove from the oven. Let cool for 1 minute.

Transfer to a wire rack and let cool.

Peanut Butter Pie

I thought that I would do my own twist (version) of Wilber's Peanut Butter Pie. The peanut butter has to be to your taste.

1 Oreo pie crust
1 1/4 to 1 1/2 cups creamy peanut butter
1 8-ounce cream cheese, softened
1/2 cup milk
1 cup powdered sugar
1/2 tub of 8 oz Cool Whip, unthawed
flaked coconut
Hershey's chocolate syrup (optional)
sprinkles (optional)

In a mixing bowl, cream together peanut butter, cream cheese, milk, and powdered sugar. Pour the mixture into the pie crust. Put in 1/2 of the tub of Cool Whip. Top with flaked coconut, zig zags of chocolate syrup, and add sprinkles to your liking.

Peanut Butter Rice Crispies Bars

This is a recipe that I came up with. You could add anything to this recipe to your own judgment. Feel free to play around with it.

4 tablespoons butter or margarine
1 bag (10 oz) jet-puffed miniature marshmallows
1 1/4 cups creamy peanut butter
1 tsp. vanilla
6 cups rice crispies

In a pan, melt the butter or margarine and marshmallows till it is creamy. Add the rest of the ingredients. Add the rice crispies mixture into a 9x9 or 9x13 pan and cover it up for 2 to 4 hours. Eat.

Rice Crispy Chocolate - Butterscotch Clusters

You can replace the butterscotch chips with chocolate chips, if you like. It's whatever you are in the mood for.
I (Sandy) believe by adding 1 to 1 1/2 cups creamy peanut butter to this, you could make these as cookies.
Sarah Scott suggested Cheerios and/or Cap'n Crunch to replace the rice crispies.

1 cup sugar
1/2 teaspoon salt
1 teaspoon vanilla
1/2 cup (1 stick) butter or margarine
1/2 cup milk
1 package chocolate chips

In a big pan, add the six ingredients together and heat on low heat until it melts. When not using the chocolate chips and want to leave them out, use the peanut butter. Mix well. Remove from the heat. Mix these ingredients together with this:

1 package butterscotch chips
4 to 6 cups rice crispies (Could use Cheerios or Cap'n Crunch)
2 cups unsalted peanuts

1. Combine the last three ingredients. Mix well.
2. Butter a 9x13 inch pan and add the ingredients.

Note: When making these as cookies, drop by large spoonfuls onto wax paper, then let stand until firm.

Store in an airtight container. Serves roughly 12 to 15. It all depends on the servings. You may get more.

Ritz Peanut Butter Chocolate Crackers

1 box Ritz crackers or club crackers
1/2 to 1 cup creamy peanut butter
1 package chocolate chips or peanut butter chips
1/4 teaspoon vanilla, optional

1. In a saucepan mix peanut butter, chocolate chips, or peanut butter chips, and optional vanilla. Mix well until the ingredients are melted.
2. Add the chocolate mixture onto a cracker and add another cracker to the top (like a sandwich). Add crackers to an container.

This is a recipe that I came up with two to three months ago.

Toffee Bars
This is a hit with the school kids, friends and family.

1 3/4 cups all-purpose flour
1/2 cup sugar
1/2 cup packed brown sugar
1 teaspoon ground cinnamon
1/4 to 1/2 teaspoon ground nutmeg
1/4 to 1/2 teaspoon ground ginger
1 cup (2 sticks) butter or margarine, softened
1 to 2 egg(s)
1 teaspoon vanilla extract
1 1/2 cups semi-sweet chocolate chips
3/4 cups finely chopped pecans or your choice of nuts

1. Preheat oven to 325 degrees.
2. In a large bowl combine flour, sugars, cinnamon, nutmeg and ginger. Mix well. Using an electric mixer add butter, egg(s) and vanilla. Beat on a low to medium speed until the dough holds together.
3. Grease or spray an 15 x 10 inch jelly roll pan. Add the dough and press well into the pan. Bake for 25 minutes or until lightly browned.
4. Immediately sprinkle with chocolate chips; let stand for 5 minutes. Spread chocolate evenly over top; sprinkle with pecans or your choice of nuts. Cut into bars while warm.

German Coffee Cake

2 stick margarine, softened
1 cup sugar
4 - 6 eggs
2 - 3 teaspoons vanilla
1/2 cup milk
3 lemon rinds, grated of the 3 and squeeze from 2 of the lemons
4 cups flour
1 package (12 ounce) Nestle's chocolate chips

1. Preheat oven to 350 degrees.
2. Lightly spray a bundt pan. In a mixing bowl combine margarine, sugar and eggs and mix with an electric mixer. Add chocolate chips and mix well with a spoon. Add the dough to the pan.
3. Bake for 45 minutes to 1 hour or until toothpick inserted in the middle comes out clean.

Peanut Butter Homemade Brownie Mix

1 cup sugar
1/2 cup all-purpose flour
1/3 cup Hershey's cocoa (I used natural unsweetened)
1/4 teaspoon salt
1/4 teaspoon baking powder

Store the above five ingredients in a plastic bag or an Mason jar. When it comes to baking these brownies add these ingredients:

2 eggs
1/2 cup vegetable oil
1 teaspoon vanilla
1 cup creamy peanut butter
1/2 to 1 cup nuts of your choice, optional

1. Preheat oven to 350 degrees.
2. In a large bowl mix the dry ingredients together. Add the eggs, vegetable oil, vanilla, peanut butter, and optional nuts. Mix well. Lightly spray an 8 x 8 or 9 x 9 inch pan, add the dough, and bake for 25 to 30 minutes.

Wilbur's Peanut Butter Pie

1 8-ounce cream cheese
3/4 cup creamy peanut butter (I Used 1 1/8 Cup)
1 cup powdered sugar
1/2 cup milk
3/4 cup (3/25) of 8 oz. tub Cool Whip
1 graham cracker pie crust

1. Beat cream cheese and peanut butter till smooth.
2. Add powdered sugar and milk till smooth.
3. Make sure that the cool whip is unthawed. Mix in the cool whip. Beat until smooth. Pour into graham pie crust.
4. Put the pie into the freezer overnight to set up, or only an hour. Add Reese's Peanut Butter Cups as decoration.

Fruit Cocktail Jell-O

4 boxes (3 ounces) orange Jell-O
4 cups water
3 cans (15 ounces) fruit cocktail, save the juice

1. In a pan add the water. Let the water come to a boil. In a bowl add the boiling water to the gelatin mix. Stir for 2 minutes or until completely dissolved.
2. Take a measuring cup and add the juice from the fruit cocktail (Should get about 1/2 cup of the juice from the fruit cocktail) and fill the rest with cold water. Add the fruit cocktail to the bowl and mix well.

Refrigerate until it's firm.

SOUPS

Potato Soup

4 small or medium potatoes, sliced fine
1 small onion, diced fine
3 celery sticks, diced fine
broth from turkey, or enough water to cover the ingredients
butter
salt and pepper

Add the above ingredients to a big saucepan. Bring to a boil, then simmer roughly 25 to 30 minutes.

Turkey Noodle Soup

leftover turkey
half of an onion, diced
3 to 4 sticks of celery, diced
water
salt and pepper
butter
2 cubes chicken cubes
1 1/2 cups egg noodles

In an big enough bowl add the leftover turkey, onion, celery, enough water. Season with salt, pepper and two tablespoons butter. Bring to a boil, add the chicken cubes and egg noodles. Cook the noodles according to directions from the noodle package.

Cucumber Chicken Soup

1 medium cucumber, peeled
2 cans (10 1/4 each) condensed cream of chicken soup
1 can regular milk
3 pieces of chicken
1 small onion, diced fine
1 small green pepper, diced fine (optional)
salt and pepper

1. Cut 8 slices off from the cucumber and reserve the rest for garnish. Chop the remaining cucumber.
2. In big pan boil the chicken, season with salt and pepper till it comes to a boil (Could add a little of butter). Once it comes to a boil bring out the chicken and cut or slice (to your liking). Once chicken is done put it back in the pan and boil for an extra 15 to 20 minutes. Drain the water from the chicken. Add the chicken back into the pan, add the soups, milk, onion and optional green pepper. Boil for 15 to 25 minutes.
3. Pour into serving bowls and garnish with the reserved cucumbers.

Turkey Potato Soup

As long you have leftover turkey, use the dark meat. It turns out better and it has a good flavor to it.

1/2 of the turkey
4 medium potatoes, peeled and sliced fine
1/2 onion from a medium onion, diced fine
3 to 4 sticks celery
1 spoon butter
2 cubes chicken broth
water
salt and pepper

In a kettle, add the turkey, potatoes, onion, celery, enough water, season with salt and pepper, and add butter. Let it come to a boil, and add the chicken cubes.

SNACKS

Sandy's Cheese Wolf Dip

1 to 1 1/2 pounds ground beef
1 can (15 oz) Wolf brand chili, no beans
1 package chili seasoning mix
1 jar salsa con queso
1/2 jar mild, medium or hot salsa
tortillas or nacho chips

1. Brown the ground beef. Season with salt and pepper. Drain the excess fat. Add the rest of the ingredients to the pan and cook for 10 to 15 minutes longer. Add the dip into a bowl.
2. Use either tortilla or nacho chips. Dip!

Sandy's Hormel Chili Dip

1 1/2 pounds ground beef
1 small onion, diced (optional)
1 package chili seasoning mix
1 can (15 oz) Hormel chili with no beans
1 jar (15.5 oz) salsa con queso
1/2 jar mild, medium or hot salsa
tortilla or nacho chips

1. Brown ground beef and optional onion. Drain the excess fat. Add the chili seasoning mix and Hormel chili. Let it cook for about 5 minutes or until hot.
2. Pour both salsas into an microwave bowl and heat for up to 2 minutes. Add the meat mixture to the salsa.
3. Use either tortilla or nacho chips. Dip!

Fiesta Dip

1 pound ground beef
1 package taco seasoning
1 can refried beans
1 jar (15.5 oz.) mild, medium or hot salsa con queso
1/2 jar mild, medium or hot salsa
tortilla or nacho chips

1. Brown the ground beef. Drain the excess fat. Add the taco seasoning and the refried beans.
2. Add the salsa con queso and the salsa to the meat mixture and cook till it simmers. Mix well. Add to a bowl and serve.
3. Use either tortilla or nacho chips. Dip!

Veggie Dip

½ to 1 cup Miracle Whip or mayo
1 package Hidden Valley Ranch dressing
1 teaspoon garlic powder
½ teaspoon lemon pepper
Your choice of vegetables (pickles, carrots, celery, etc.)

In a big enough bowl add the four ingredients and mix well. Dip with pickles, carrots, celery or whichever vegetables you like.

Chex Party Mix

You can always add other ingredients to your liking.

1 box corn chex
1 box rice chex
1 box wheat chex
1 box cheerios
1 pound (1 jar) salted or unsalted peanuts
1 bag pretzels
1 bag M&M's, optional
1 tablespoon garlic powder
1 stick of butter or margarine, melted

In a big enough bowl add all of the ingredients together. Or you could add all of the ingredients into a big zip lock bag and shake well.

Gold Seasoned Crackers

1 package goldfish crackers
2 bags oyster crackers
1/2 cup warm oil
1 package original Hidden Valley ranch dressing
2 teaspoons garlic powder
1 teaspoon lemon pepper
1 teaspoon dill weed

1. In a container mix together the crackers and sprinkle the dry ingredients over the top ingredients.
2. Pour the warm oil over the crackers. Shake well.
3. Store in an air-tight container.

Seasoned Crackers

2 bags (12 oz) oyster crackers
1 cup oil
1 package original Hidden Valley ranch dressing
2 teaspoons garlic powder
1 teaspoon dill weed
1/2 teaspoon onion powder
1 teaspoon lemon pepper

1. In a container mix together the crackers and sprinkle the dry ingredients over the crackers.
2. Pour warm oil over the crackers. Mix until absorbed!
3. Store in an airtight container. Let set overnight.

The Original Cracker Seasoned Mix

When you have crackers along with Hidden Valley Ranch Dressing and any other ingredients, then you'll have your mix.

4 containers (8.0 oz) flavored crackers (vegetable flavored, sour cream & onion flavored, or other flavored crackers)
1 package original Hidden Valley Ranch Dressing
2 teaspoons garlic powder
1 teaspoon lemon pepper
1 teaspoon dill weed
1 to 1½ cups peanuts
½ bag of pretzels
½ cup oil

1. In a big bowl mix together the crackers, peanuts, pretzels, and the dry ingredients.
2. Pour the warm oil over the ingredients and shake well.
3. Store in an air tight container.

Deviled Eggs

These tends to go quickly around the Fourth of July cookouts. We tend to adjust the Miracle Whip, mustard, and salt, depending on how many yolks we get.

12 hard cooked eggs
2 heaping miracle whip or mayo or to taste
mustard to your liking
salt to your liking
vinegar, optional
paprika or parsley, optional

Cut the eggs long ways. Remove the yolks and set them into a bowl and set aside. Mash the yolks, add the miracle whip or mayo, mustard, salt and optional vinegar. Mix well. Stuff the yolk into the eggs and place them into the egg tray. If desired garnish with paprika or parsley.

Shandi Hart

Spaghetti Sauce

1 1/2 pounds ground beef
1 large onion, diced fine
1 large green pepper, diced fine
little water
1 can tomato paste
1 can tomato sauce
1 envelope spaghetti sauce mix
1 can diced tomatoes
spaghetti noodles

1. In an skillet brown ground beef, onion, green pepper and a little bit of water. Drain the excess fat.
2. Add tomato paste and tomato sauce to the meat and heart up. Add the envelope of spaghetti sauce mix and add diced tomatoes. Add to drained cooked spaghetti noodles.

Carole Cline, Melleigha Nichols, Shandi Hart, Kodie M. Masoner and Christohper Hale, this is your Grandpa Cline's recipe. Kelly Cline, I know that I already gave you the recipe.

Sandy's Spicy Tomato Sauce

Here is a sauce that I came up with last week. I think that you might like it.

1 medium onion, diced or a package of onion mix
1 tsp. garlic powder
1/2 cup cracker crumbs or bread crumbs
1/2 teaspoon salt
1/2 teaspoon black pepper
1/2 teaspoon liquid smoke or Worcestershire sauce
1 small or medium tomato sauce
other ingredients to your taste

1. In an big enough bowl, add all of the ingredients together. Mix well.
2. Pour over meatballs.

Classic Homemade Barbecue Sauce

1 cup ketchup
2 tablespoons liquid smoke or worcestershire sauce
1 tablespoon sugar or 1/2 cup packed brown sugar
1 package onion soup mix
1/2 teaspoon garlic powder
Cooked meatballs

1. Have the meatballs in a cooking dish. In a sauce pan, combine ketchup, liquid smoke or worcestershire sauce, sugar or brown sugar, onion soup mix, and garlic powder. When it comes to a boil, take the pan off the burner and pour the sauce over the meatballs.
2. Bake for 15 to 20 minutes or to your liking.

Seasoning Blend

This is good for all-purpose seasoning. This can go into batter for fish tacos (any type of tacos of your choice) or it could be used as a seasoning for poultry, pork, beef, lamb, roast and even for other cooking methods. Could use this seasoning when roasting and or grilling. You could change ingredients to your desire.

1/4 cup garlic powder
1/4 cup onion powder
1/4 cup seasoning salt or meat tenderizer
1/4 cup black pepper
1/8 cup salt
1/4 teaspoon cayenne pepper
could add other seasonings to your desire

In a big enough bowl combine all the ingredients. Mix well. Add the seasoning to an air-tight container (bowl) or shaker. Store in an dark place. Keeps for up to 6 months.

Makes 1 to 1 1/2 cups

Julie Powell Casey

Good Gravy

1 1/2 pounds ground beef
salt and pepper
1/4 to 1/2 cup all-purpose flour
milk

Brown the ground beef and season with salt and pepper. Drain the grease. Add the flour, enough milk, and season with salt and pepper. Stir till it gets thick, or to your liking.

Breads

Do you hate going to the store and they don't have the breads that you tend to buy? As long that they have the bread, or if it's on sale, stock up. Freeze the loaves of breads in the freezer. When ready to have the bread, bring out a loaf. I (Sandy) learned this from Chris.

wheat or white bread
hot dog buns
hamburger buns

1. Buy amount of bread, hot dog buns and hamburger buns and put them into the freezer.
2. Bring bread, hot dog buns and hamburger buns out a day in advance.

ABOUT THE AUTHOR

Sandy Smith grew up in Savannah, Missouri.

She tends to enjoy writing and cooking.

Made in the USA
Columbia, SC
29 December 2017